Foster Their Imagination

A Creative Journal for Kids

Activinotes

Activinotes

DAILY JOURNALS, PLANNERS, NOTEBOOKS AND OTHER BLANK BOOKS

Creative Journal

of

_____

My Simple Thought and Imagination

Scribble Fun

My Simple Thought and Imagination

Scribble Fun

My Simple Thought and Imagination

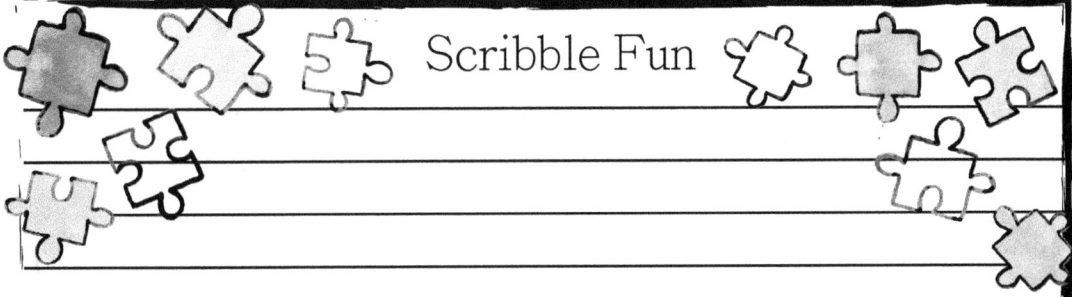

Scribble Fun

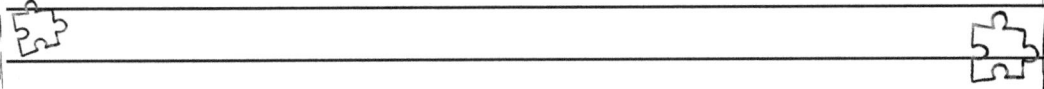

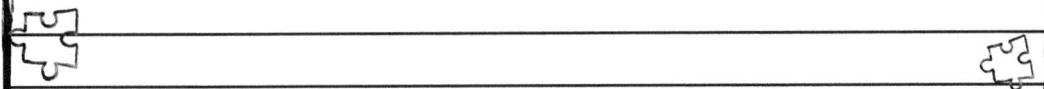

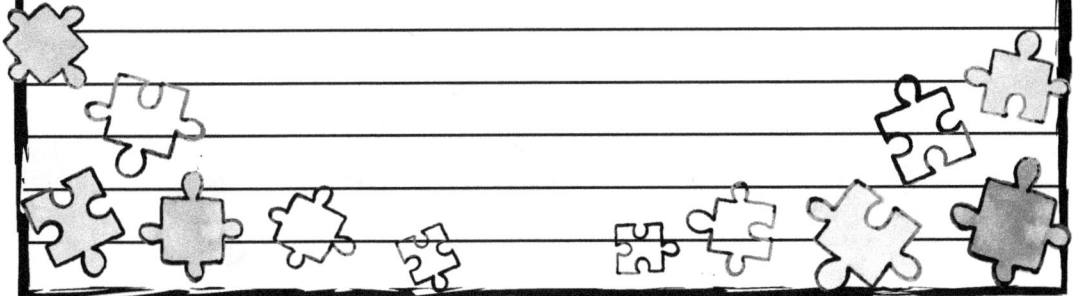

My Simple Thought and Imagination

Scribble Fun

My Simple Thought and Imagination

Scribble Fun

My Simple Thought and Imagination

Scribble Fun

My Simple Thought and Imagination

Scribble Fun

My Simple Thought and Imagination

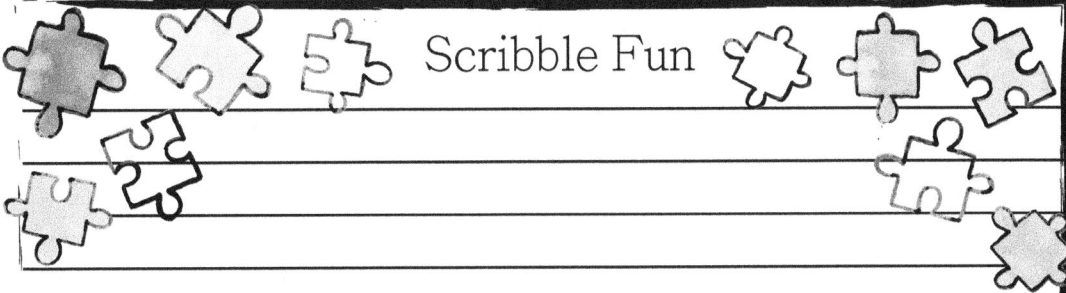

Scribble Fun

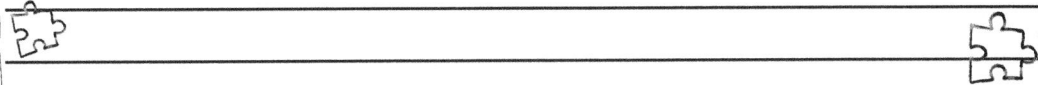

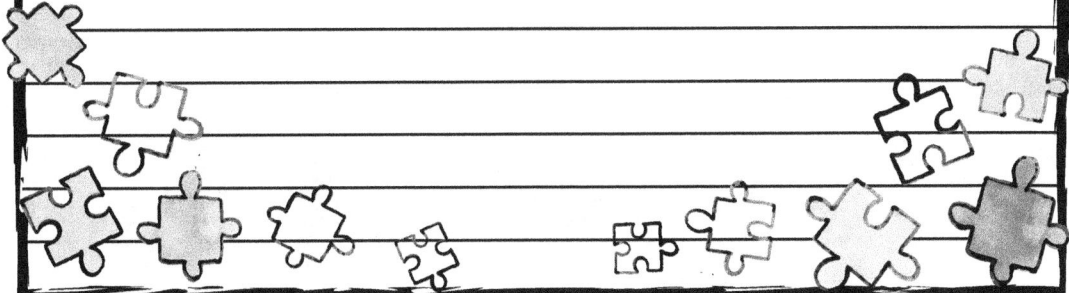

My Simple Thought and Imagination

Scribble Fun

My Simple Thought and Imagination

Scribble Fun

My Simple Thought and Imagination

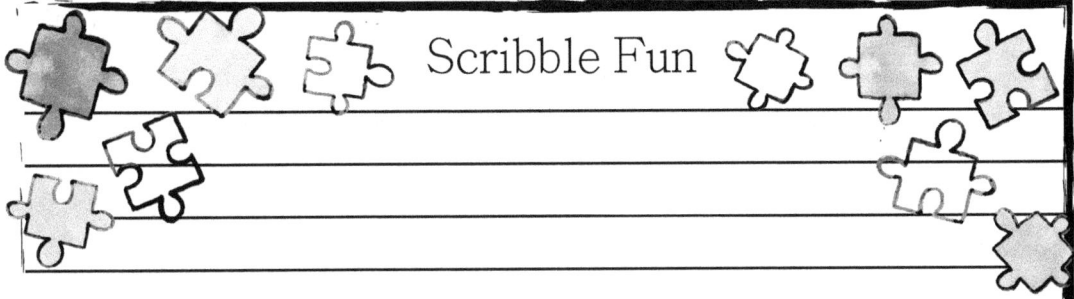

Scribble Fun

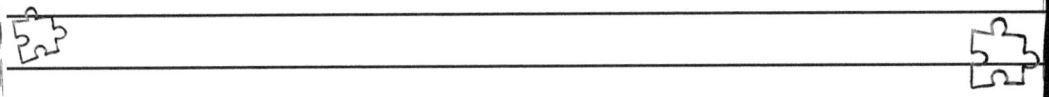

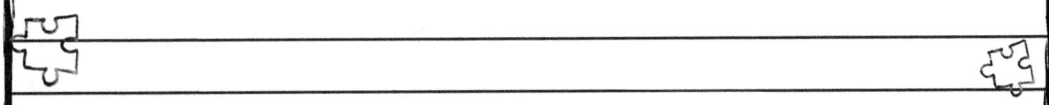

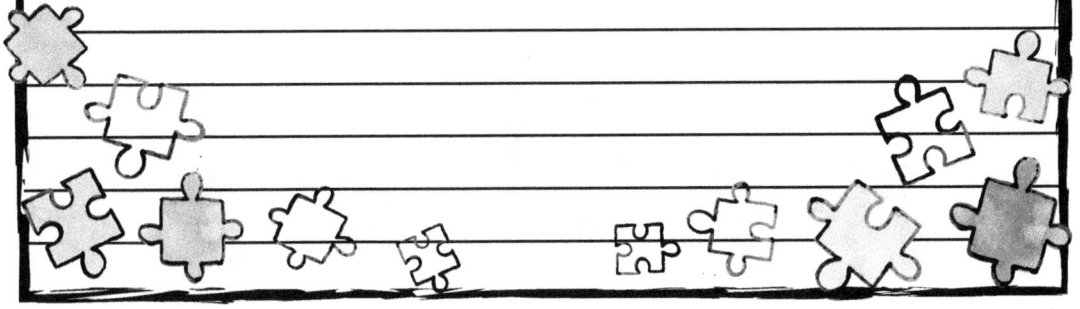

My Simple Thought and Imagination

Scribble Fun

My Simple Thought and Imagination

Scribble Fun

My Simple Thought and Imagination

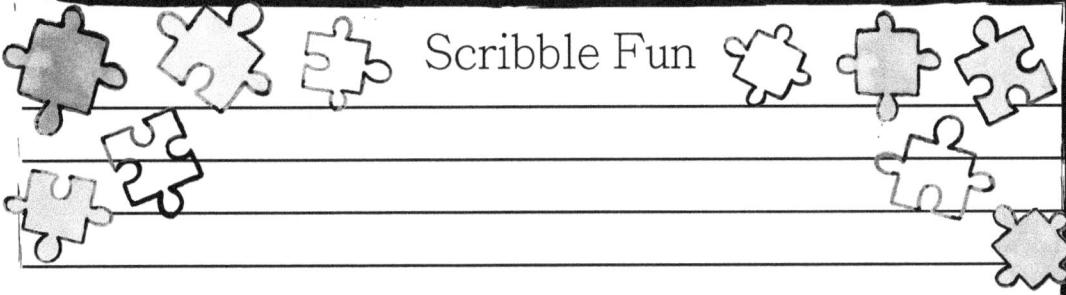

Scribble Fun

My Simple Thought and Imagination

Scribble Fun

My Simple Thought and Imagination

Scribble Fun

My Simple Thought and Imagination

Scribble Fun

My Simple Thought and Imagination

Scribble Fun

My Simple Thought and Imagination

Scribble Fun

My Simple Thought and Imagination

Scribble Fun

My Simple Thought and Imagination

Scribble Fun

My Simple Thought and Imagination

Scribble Fun

My Simple Thought and Imagination

Scribble Fun

My Simple Thought and Imagination

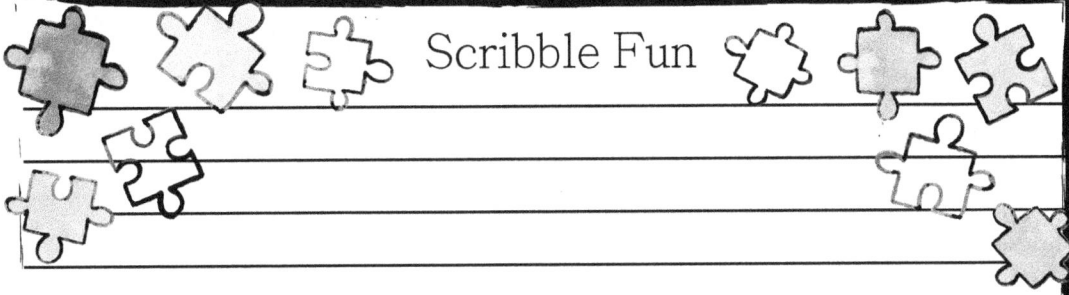

Scribble Fun

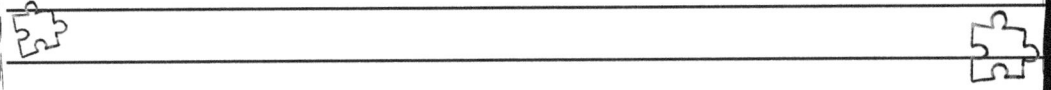

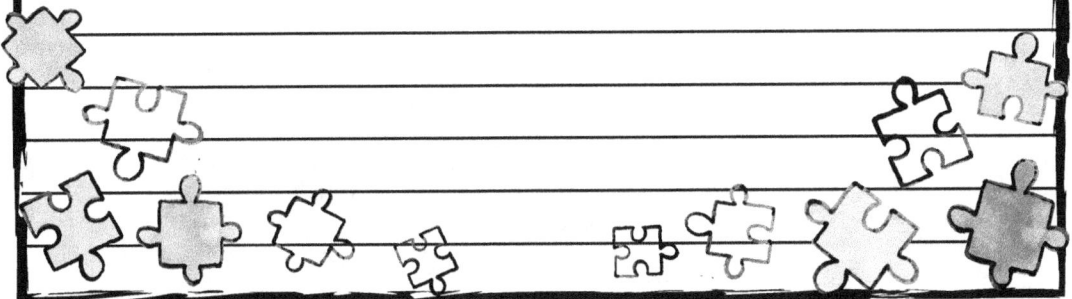

My Simple Thought and Imagination

Scribble Fun

My Simple Thought and Imagination

Scribble Fun

My Simple Thought and Imagination

Scribble Fun

My Simple Thought and Imagination

Scribble Fun

My Simple Thought and Imagination

Scribble Fun

My Simple Thought and Imagination

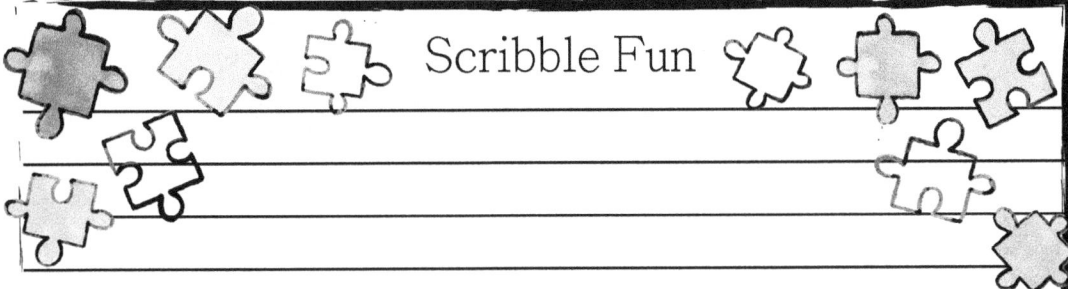

Scribble Fun

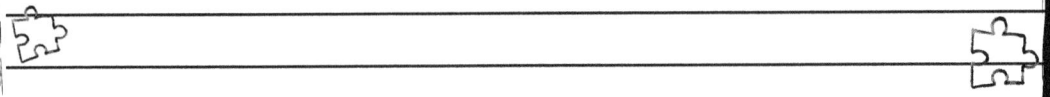

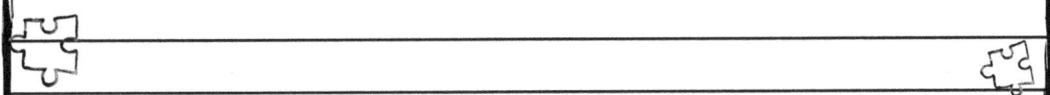

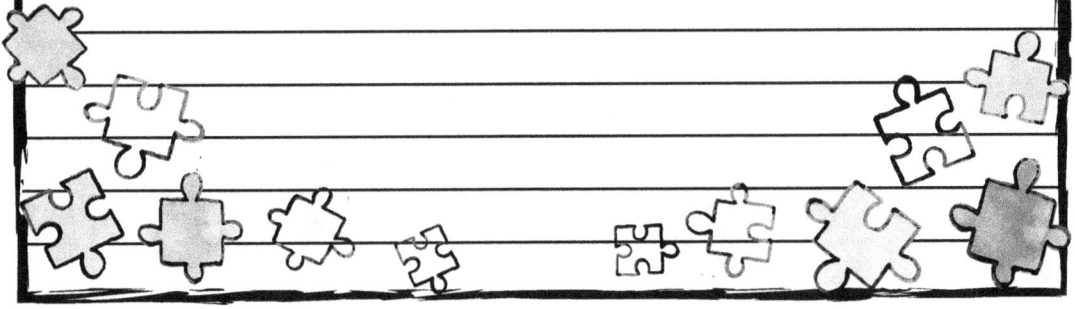

My Simple Thought and Imagination

Scribble Fun

My Simple Thought and Imagination

Scribble Fun

My Simple Thought and Imagination

Scribble Fun

My Simple Thought and Imagination

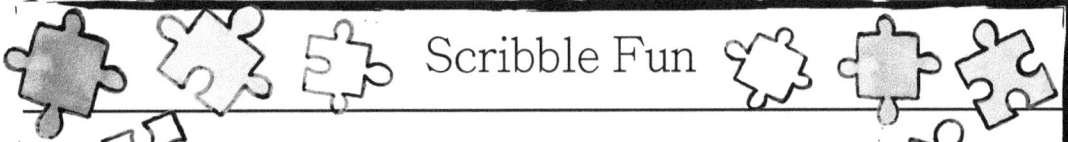

Scribble Fun

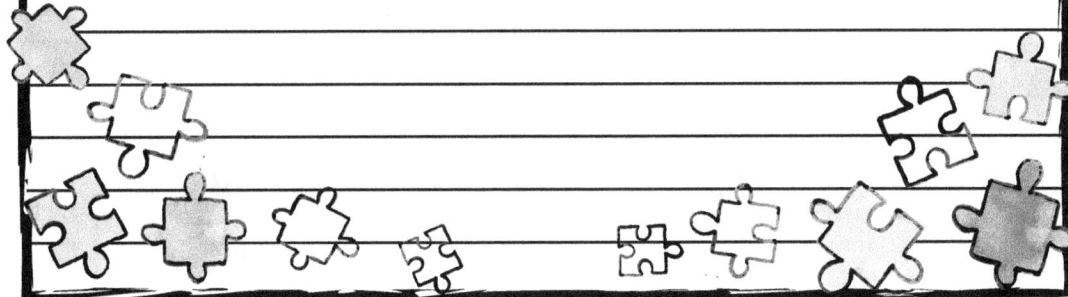

My Simple Thought and Imagination

Scribble Fun

My Simple Thought and Imagination

Scribble Fun

My Simple Thought and Imagination

Scribble Fun

My Simple Thought and Imagination

Scribble Fun

My Simple Thought and Imagination

Scribble Fun

My Simple Thought and Imagination

Scribble Fun

My Simple Thought and Imagination

Scribble Fun

My Simple Thought and Imagination

Scribble Fun

My Simple Thought and Imagination

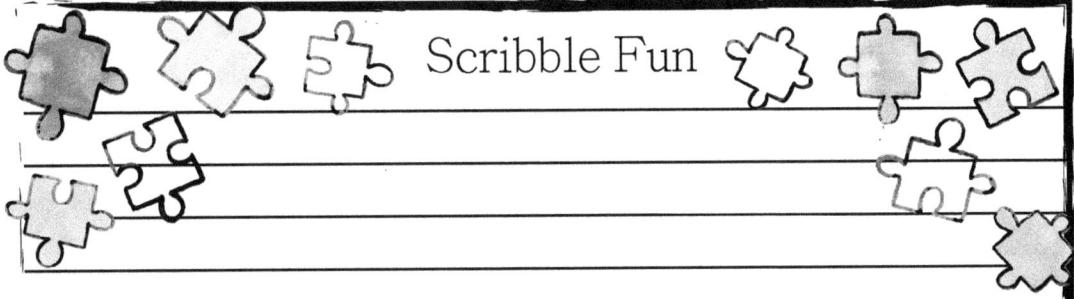

Scribble Fun

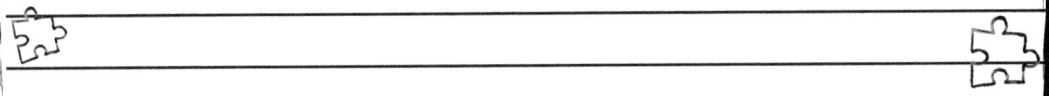

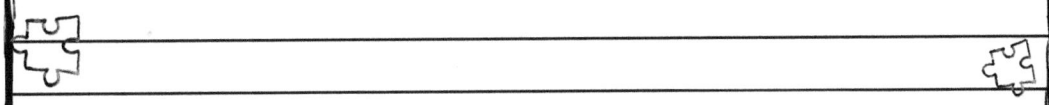

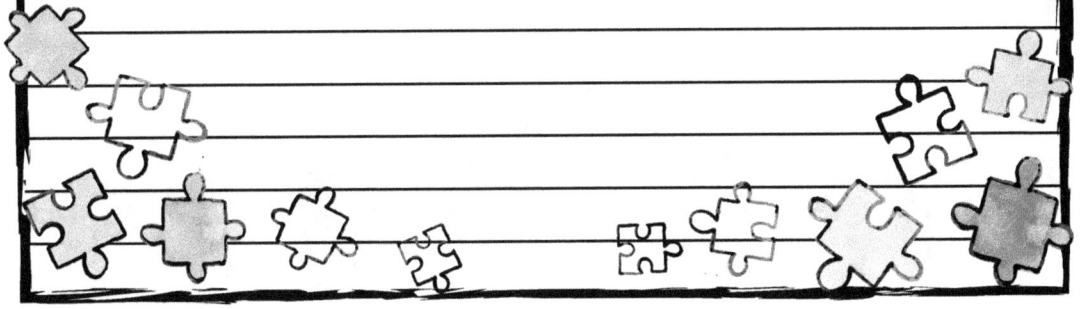

My Simple Thought and Imagination

Scribble Fun

My Simple Thought and Imagination

Scribble Fun

My Simple Thought and Imagination

Scribble Fun

My Simple Thought and Imagination

Scribble Fun

My Simple Thought and Imagination

Scribble Fun

My Simple Thought and Imagination

Scribble Fun

My Simple Thought and Imagination

Scribble Fun

My Simple Thought and Imagination

Scribble Fun